<u>28</u>

Written by: Amber Ocean

Free to love,
Love to live,
Live to love,
Love is this.

This book, my first book,

I dedicate to my amazing friend.
Without him, I doubt if I would have ever picked up a pen.
Chasen K. Marshall, I thank God for you.

To the reader, I thank you for reading.
See this book as a glimpse of my journey through the years,
Expressed through my thoughts, my feelings, and my words.
Hope you enjoy.

XOXO ~Amber Ocean

AMBER- jewel, valuable, desirable, natural beauty

OCEAN- fierce, deep, turmoil, peace, intricate, wild, strong, powerful, beautiful, unforgettable, life, free

Just a few words to describe me.

You and Me

I USED TO LOVE YOU
NOTHING USED TO COME BEFORE YOU
I GUESS I LOST YOU
SOMEWHERE BETWEEN THE HE SAY AND SHE SAY
YOU WERE ALL THAT I USED TO SEE
ALL THAT I WANTED TO BE
YOU WERE ME
NOW, I PRETEND LIKE I DON'T EVEN KNOW YOU
LIKE WE NEVER WERE
I TREAT YOU LIKE,
I CAN EXIST ALONE WITH JUST ME
I NEED YOU
I AM FOOLING NO ONE BUT MYSELF
PEOPLE FROM LONG AGO KNEW THAT YOU AND ME
WAS THE REAL THING
BUT I PUSHED YOU AWAY
BY PUTTING EVERYTHING BETWEEN ME AND YOU
THE NEW PEOPLE IN MY LIFE DON'T EVEN KNOW YOU EXIST TO ME
AND YOU ARE MY GREATEST GIFT
YOU ARE BEAUTIFUL
THE ONLY ONE WHO TRULY UNDERSTANDS ME
I FEEL SO OFF-CENTERED AND UNBALANCED
WITHOUT YOU
YOU GIVE ME EVERYTHING THAT I AM LOOKING FOR,
NOW I REALIZE THAT
MY PEACE, MY JOY, MY CONFIDENCE,
THAT WAS ALL YOU
AND NOW SINCE WE DON'T TALK,
MY HEAD IS DOWN WHEN I WALK,

AND YOU KNOW THAT AIN'T ME
I'M GETTING OLD AND GRAY
MY CLOTHES DON'T FIT THE SAME
NOT ONLY DID I GAIN SOME WEIGHT,
I GAINED SOME SELF HATE
I PUT OTHERS BEFORE YOU,
AND THAT'S WHERE THE PROBLEM LIES
BECAUSE THOSE OTHERS PUT OTHERS BEFORE ME
AND I'M STILL HERE
STUCK
LIFE IS MOVING ON WITHOUT ME
NO DIRECTION
I USED TO BE SO HIGH ON LIFE WITH YOU
YOU ALLOWED ME TO BELIEVE IN MY DREAMS
BELIEVE IN ME
I DON'T LIKE WHERE I'M AT
AND I KNOW IF I DONT HOLD ON TO YOU NOW,
YOU COULD BE GONE FOR GOOD
AND I JUST CAN'T HAVE THAT
WHAT I'M SAYING IS
I WANT YOU BACK
I WANT US BACK
I WANT YOU TO BE THE ONE CONSISTANTLY ON MY MIND
I WANT US TO BE THE BEST
LET GO OF ALL THE REST AND LET'S DO THIS
I WANT US TO BE BIGGER THAN I COULD HAVE EVER IMAGINED
I WANT US NEVER TO BE APARTAGAIN
I WANT MY WORDS BACK
MY MELODIES BACK
I WANT THAT SONG IN MY HEART BACK
I NEED YOU,

SO IM GOING TO DO WHATEVER IT IS TO KEEP YOU
POETRY, LYRICS, SONGS
YOU ARE THE REAL ME
I LOVE YOU

THANK YOU

I thank you,
I thank you for taking a chance on me
For loving me
And for being a friend to me
I thank you for believing in me
For showing me
For taking a part of the molding of me
For you being a listening ear
For you being you
For you being here
I thank you
You are sweet and amazing
Your voice is
Strong and liberating
Speech of a king
Countenance of a dream
I've watched you
Watch me
As I watch you
Surely, become the man
You were created to be
My heart is thankful for thee
You have always kept me in awe
Forever you will be in my heart
I'll owe you for life
It is you who gave birth to the me who writes
I love you so much
Chasen K. Marshall
Thank You

Here

I'm here in this place of uncertainty
of complacency, insecurity
Hurt, shame
You would never know it, because I mask my pain
with wild nights and hypocrisy
a bad attitude and negativity
fitting in comfortably and settling for mediocrity
My nerves are bad
Crazy thoughts on why, and what happened to me?
My mind is covered in black erasing all memories
I didn't use to be this way, How did I get here?
Today I address these issues
Today I let them go
I came from a life
where sugar coating was the way to go
Where new things erased how you really feel
I come from a place where
the one who gave me life couldn't even love me
Can walk by me in the streets today and wouldn't even know me
I come from a life where
having an opinion never even mattered
where being different trying new things you were considered a disaster
I grew up in a home where even though I had everything
materialistically,
it meant nothing to me because I had no one to hug me
No daddy to say he loved me
I grew up having ass and titties, big lips, and every man around me
wanted to put his hands on my hips
I grew up keeping a secret, that a particular someone

really took a liking to me, liked to play in my privacy
All of this before I was even 15
I grew up where the girls around me couldn't stand me,
so they name called and gossiped and never really knew me
I grew up believing that any attention was good attention,
even if they had bad intentions
I learned that to even get a piece of the love I knew I was missing,
I would have to give something up and pass out more than
just some kisses
As I grew older I used my body to pay for the things I knew money
couldn't buy
By 21, I had become everything I had said I wasn't
a hoe, a prostitute
I has so high on the bullshit I was injecting into me,
I didn't even realize that all of that was just a temporary fix
I had nowhere to turn
Though I was young, I felt so old
So lonely, so cold
I decided to really give this thing my friends told me about a try
I felt what love was for the first time
I realized that God loves me, yea, me, I
I've changed I don't do the same things
I pray now, I listen before speak
He loved me at my worst the least I can do is live at my best
So I'm letting go right now of all that old mess
I'm forgiving myself I'm starting fresh
I've been rejuvenated with grace
My bitterness has been removed, my mouth has a sweeter taste
My eyes see beauty that I had never known before
I appreciate the things around me
I finding out what joy is more and more

I let go of my past this day, I step out, I am free to live
I've been given gifts, I've been created to do more, To be better
I believe I was saved to say,
No matter what it looks like, No matter what you think or thought,
It doesn't matter anymore
The past is past and the bad only lasts how long you make it
Live today, Change now, Today, Be better today

Talk to Me

Past Love
More Real to me than others
Significant
I compare you not to the ones before you
I see you
As though, I am presented with
Something new
Something fresh
As the next step
I've never known a soul like you
loving every part
down to the soles of you
happiness you bring
WOW
Now I've become in awe of you
I see you sometimes before you see me
and I watch closely
wondering if you'd ever find me
The other side of you
brings complexity to the mind
My mind wonders
and I become corrupt in your ways
You make me want to...
You, confuse me at times
about simple shit
like telling me
you go call me
Right, Right Back
and you don't

Like, "What is that?
"What are you doing?"
like sometimes,
We can't go an hour
without talking to each other
Then you flip it,
like two days without one another
and that doesn't seem to bother you
I worry about you
Can't leave you,
because you'd go crazy
You can't function without me
Or so you say
cause I ain't talked to you all day
You are my best friend,
but you keeping messing with me
If it ain't somebody else
Then, "What is it?"
"What am I doing wrong?"
You talk to me about everything else
You say I don't understand
But,
You aren't saying anything
for me to comprehend
So I'ma give you some space
Whatever it is
I hope you are okay
Remember I love you
And I'm here when you need me

Crazy

When I see you, I don't see me-
When I hear us, I don't see we-
You alone have caused my head to hurt, my eyes to cry,
my heart to break-
All because, it didn't have to be this way-
The shit that went down between us was foolish, ridiculous-
The shit you did to me was ruthless-
I can't believe the person that I had representing the other half of me,
would allow negativity, and stupidity-
Reduce oneself to the equivalent, to just another hoe off the street-
I gave you all of me-That equals everything-
Surpassed your expectations-
Worked hard to make sure you/us/I/we were happy-
But I guess my best wasn't good enough for you-
You have always known how to fuck some shit up-
You walk around like your shit don't stank-
And it does-
Call it crazy-
But I loved that smell of you-
Love not only makes you blind,
But it allows you to tolerate some foul smelling shit-
Makes it smell good-
But now, I smell shit-
I see now it ain't me, but it's you-
Your fucked up attitude, how ungrateful you are-
And how big of a mistake and waste of time you are-
There I was, trying to do the right thing
-Fully loving you-
It was good in the beginning-

It always is-
One thing I know fa'sho now-
It's a mutha Fker when it ends

Now

I can honestly say love has stretched me sideways.
Hurt has pulled me around.
Shame has knocked me down.
Where do I go from here?
I'm lost.
I'm at this point everything is moving so fast,
but my life is going unbelievably slow.
I lost all control.
I don't know my right from left.
Don't know which next turn is correct.
I'm scattered.
Alone.
Afraid.
Sad.
But filled with rage, because what I want and what the heart needs,
What my eyes see and the reality of the situation,
Aren't making any sense.
Nothing is connecting.
I feel a strong disconnect from the outside world.
I have no trust.
No loyalty.
No peace.
There's no proof or evidence of me occupying space.
I need something more.

To: My Biological Father

Who creates life and then takes it away?
I'm not dead
But there is hole in my heart
You put it there
Incomplete
Not that I needed you
But I did,
You were supposed to be
The one I first fell in love with
The one I could come to about anything
You were supposed to be the one that made me believe
That I was beautiful, But you weren't there
You never have been
Where were you?
What were you doing that was so important that you couldn't love me?
I can't even remember the last time I saw you
Don't even really know what you look like
What your voice sounds like
I have nothing positive to say about you
But
Thank you
You leaving me
Us, we, them too
Allowed me to suffer
Become low, dark
Caused me to feel insignificant
Less than
Question my purpose for living
The one who was supposed to love me didn't

You,
Or the lack there of
caused me to give up on me
I tried to get closer to you
A prostitute that was me
Selling sex for just a little time that I couldn't get from you
My backside got me a lot
My mouth got me more
I was winning
But since my soul was in it,
I had already lost before the game had begun
I did tricks for tricks,
So they could trick off me
But I was only fooling myself
No amount of money is worth my honey
You had me feeling ugly
I never thought I was pretty
That was only for the girls who had one of you in their life
Crazy and defeated, angry
Shirt soaked from leaked hurt
God whispered something to me
Told me, He loved me
I didn't know what that was, couldn't see how he could
He showed me
He gave me peace
I don't understand anything from the past
I'll probably never get any questions I have for you answered
Probably never see you again
I have peace with that
I forgave myself for hating you the way I did
I feel sorry for you

Because you are not around to see the beautiful woman I have become
Inside and out
I'm smart and people tell me I'm funny
They say I kind of act like you
But I'll never know
I am amazing and I am happy
And people love me for me
I'm doing things
I made myself believe I couldn't
So I do thank you
I thank you for my little sister
If you think I'm something,
She is something special
And I thank you for my three brothers, who I know love me
They say I'm beautiful,
And it means the world to me
I know what love is now
Something that isn't forced
You can't see it but you can feel it
Each day is progress for me
I decided not to allow you and your ways dictate the rest of my life
How can I allow one I don't even know
Ruin my life?
I love you, I do
I thought I could go on and hate you forever,
But I can't
I love you,
Even though you don't love me
And I forgive you for that too
I've let it go
I love myself to much to hold on

I'm now moving on
Take care of yourself

Pretty Girl

As pretty as you are,
As beautiful as you have become,
Without substance
You have nothing
Nothing to hold on to,
Nothing to remember you by,
But you have a pretty face
Even though there's millions of pretty faces,
Those same faces
Most are basic
Average at best
But who wants that
If you're like everybody then you can be replaced by anybody
Not needed
Not missed
But you got nice lips
You have to begin to pour in to your heart so you can see from your soul
So much more to life than to be blinded by opinions,
Held back by thoughts
You have to live to love
Breathe to be
See to dream
Fall in love with you
Completely
Now that's a pretty girl

Left Out

I went 55 miles an hour heading home,
tears coming down my face
Sad because us ended before we started
Love, misused in this situation
Friends, the word used in this equation
I'm stuck because where I want to be,
who we are,
and what you know, don't match
its always your way
but you don't see it
You don't get it
I can't stand your word choice
I hate your attitude
You treat me like the end of something good
Like you don't care
(tear)
It hurts my feelings
because sometimes you are not
who you make yourself out to be
You supposed to love me
but I feel like shit
I shut my mouth
I let you win
but it's my fault
I let you in
I let you get to me
I let you make me angry
Something I shouldn't do
Because you ain't even fucked yet

Found out why
Because I'm not your type
I'm not her
and I don't have what you like
but I try
I sucked your dick
because you told me to
I didn't want to
I call it my last ditch effort to get you to see
how much I really do care about you
and your feelings
and what you're going through
I smile, I laugh
I really don't know how to handle you
I guess I'm still awe of the you I met in 03
still hold on to the possibilities
I got to let it go
(tear)
I got to let you go
You should not have this effect on me
We are friends so let's keep it that way
I hate to say it,
but I need you to treat me like them other girls
You doing it so well already
I guess I like you more than I should,
think to highly of you
especially when you give me the bare minimum
Say enough to get your dick sucked,
for me to swallow your kids when you nut,
but then turn around and give the "We are friends at church hug"
Naw nigga,

there's no benefits in loving you
You don't see it
You don't get it
You don't want it
I disappoint you
I play all the games
and I lack common sense
and I'm average
I've lost
especially when I can't compare to
your love of chocolate skin
I feel so low,
so it's you that has to go
A topical acquaintance,
that's all I can offer to you
I'm done
I'm gone
Oh, not that you care
because you haven't called,
I'm home

Sweetest Thing

Pretty thang
I like it standing tall
Looking at me
One eyed monster
Vicious
All brown
Perfect
like hot chocolate
Nice size
Thick and right
I wanna sleep by it all night
love to suck on it,
so it can shine
Gleaming
Juices streaming
Fall down
in my mouth
Tastes sweet
I want it for hours
filling up my jaws
till my cheeks hurt
Then I want it in my secret place
that's already ready
just because I was looking at it
Put it in
Fill it full
Beat it up
Don't take it out
Wait

Now give it here
In my mouth
3 ounces of
Thick and rich
Cream
Swallow
Sweetest thing I've ever known,
Comes in the prettiest brown skin tone

Christopher

I honestly loved you
I did
My whole heart was in it
More than me I loved you
I still do
But it's different now
I never knew we would change
Things change, people do to,
But who would have thought there would be
No more me and you
Not that it ever was
We were officially unofficial
Because you got her and I had them
But there was no other him but you in my eyes
I kept you on a pedestal
Why?
You already tall enough
All I did was make you touch the sky
Made you my moon
And my stars
My sun
My light
My night
My wrong
My right
And you knew it too
I know you loved me too
I know you still do
But love is crazy sometimes

As great as it is
It hurts so bad
It hurts so bad that I can't love you like I want too
How you need to be
And you can't do the same for me
I guess that's why I'm prolonging the statement
That tells you the purpose of me writing to you
But before I do
Let me tell you this
My love for you was pure
Unparalleled to any love I could give another
You know what it was
When you kissed me
I felt like...
And when you looked at me
And when you laughed with me
And all that other stuff we did
Besides bust nuts
That's what I loved the most
I'm just in a place now
Where number two
doesn't work for me
Second place isn't winning
Your actions tell me what it is
I won't compete
My mind is made up
You made your decision and I respect that
But you need to know
My true heart's desire is for you to be happy
With or without me
I want you happy

Her, me, or she
I want you happy
Live your life
I told you this before
How great you are
You're amazing
You hurt me,
But I forgive you
I really do
Maybe later in life we will meet up
Reminisce on when my sweetest taste was you
Lips and your tip
And your lips again
Maybe this space will lead back to love again
Or maybe for me and you this is the end
And either way it goes,
However the cookie may crumble,
I will always love you
Bittersweet memories,
That is all I'm taking with me
So here's what I came for,
Goodbye, old friend, goodbye

Freedom

I just released the sweetest thing I've ever known
for a chance at love
For me
Sight unseen or unheard
I trade all my possessions
for a love so true
Pure and priceless
I'm giving up
what makes me up
To start over
To live natural
No make up
I live now free
with only air to breathe
And a heart that beats
Joy and Peace
and Love for me

BLACK

AS MUCH OF A LIGHT AS I AM,
YOU CONTINUE TO COVER ME
YOU HATE TO SEE ME SHINE
YOU KEEP PUTTING YOUR HANDS ON ME
I LIKE TO BELIEVE I'M BEAUTIFUL,
BUT YOU THINK I'M FULL OF MYSELF
AND IT'S YOUR JOB TO BEAT THE PRETTY OUT OF ME
NOW I'M UGLY
SELF ESTEEM GONE
EYES BLOOD SHOT RED
I LOOK IN THE MIRROR TRYING TO FIND ME
ONLY TO FIND A BLACK CIRCLE COVERING MY EYE LOOKING AT ME
I CRY
YOU SCREAM
MORE BLACK
MASCARA ON MY HANDS FROM TEARS
YOUR HANDS DRAW BACK
YOU WANT QUIET,
BUT I WANT PEACE
I WANT TO BE GREAT, YOU WANT TO BEAT ME
MORE BLACK
YOUR FIST CONNECTS TO MY CHEEK
I CAN'T EVEN BREATHE
YOU SAY I DON'T LISTEN
HOW CAN I WHEN YOU DON'T SPEAK?
MORE BLACK
ANOTHER BLOW
I'M ON THE GROUND
FADING OUT

IS THIS WHAT LOVE IS ABOUT?
IS THIS THE DREAM?
I'M SILENT
I'M LOSING STRENTGH
I'M TIRED
I'M LETTING GO
BLACK
MORE BLACK
ALL BLACK
BLACK
WHERE IS MY LIGHT?

Sometimes...

I forget how much I'm worth
Let my temporary feelings
Affect my logical thinking
My physical safety
My well being
Sometimes I over think,
Then I don't think enough
Sometimes I just wanna nut
Then it's times like this,
I just need to feel loved
Moving past what was
What came easy
What felt good
Content with comfortable
Purging my growth
Hindering my outcome
Sometimes I replace
What I know to be true
and replace those thoughts
with false prophecies
that tell me what the world thinks I should be
and forget what I was designed a created to be
Sometimes I know all this
and continue to do what I want to do
like I don't know better, like I can't do better...
Sometimes, I love others harder than I love myself
Silly because the only one that truly loves me is myself
I've got to remember my worth,
know it without any shadow of doubt,

And stop changing the price,
Regardless of who's the highest bidder

MOMMY

You have given me everything
You love me, I do know
You are crazy and mean,
But you love me
I work your nerves
And you get on mine
We are more alike than different
If you left me,
It would break my heart
You are irreplaceable
I love you
As I have grown I see everything you have done for me
And I appreciate it
I see good in you
You are phenomenal,
And at times I take you for granted
Please forgive me
Love you much mommy

A Little Letter to Jesus

I feel you pulling me near,
But I'm constantly fighting you back
I'm busy doing this and you're the only one
trying to give me that
Real and full
and all the way love
At night instead of praising thee,
I'm spending time on my knees
Pleasing those who are no good for me
I know better,
but I don't do
My life is a mess,
So I guess now I'll call you
I'm so busy doing wrong
I don't even meet you halfway
I can't even say I love you
or thank you for today
I'm greedy and I'm selfish
and you keep giving and providing
You protect me, watch me, keep me
and all I do is keep giving me out like its free
How can I even ask you for anything?
I deserve nothing,
but you continue to love me
Who am I?
I'm lost in this world of stolen identities
Jagged and torn
Hurt and insecure
words that describe me

How can this be, when I say I love you?
I don't know how much you love me
I'm giving myself halfway to you
Barely, if even at all
And you're still here loving me
more than I love myself

Seasons

I used to be happy when you called me
Used to heat up like the heat
In 2010 summer in Cali
You used to be on my mind,
but like the leaves I'm waiting to see,
Brown, green, and mahogany
You fall from that place
I put you in earlier this year
when the grass was green
You wasn't so mean in the spring.
I thought that it would be different
Now that we are here at the end of the year
We not even there yet
and I'm cold
Our love is old
and even though I want you so,
There is no love for you this winter

Newness

There something about the new
That keeps me intrigued
That keeps me wide open
Something about the new that makes me
want to impress
That makes me want to do my best
Something about the newness of you makes me
Care
Crazy because I usually don't
I want to know more about you
Makes me want to invest in you
See where this thing will go
See how good will it be before you turn old
and it becomes so easy to walk away
and I'm no longer trapped up on you
Tripping, thinking, and slipping on you
When you become dull and scratched,
bruised and tainted,
and I put you away with all my other toys
Until there is a, maybe next time, we can see if maybe we
But right now,
I love how you shining
You got such a twinkle in your eye
Your actions say you really want to be here,
so I'ma let you
I'ma let you inject me with that sweet sugar called bullshit
It's bad for you, but some can't get enough of it
Sound so good, so for a minute I'ma bask in it
Close my eyes let it sink in

only skin deep though
I'ma allow you to kiss me
let you breathe some of that
Giddy, happy shit
Some of that
Let me have some more of you, infatuation
Because I wanna like that
I think that you might can like me, like I like you
I'ma let you look at me smile at me
Put them both together and done properly
Drip dropping, swish swashing, pussy gushing all over you
Wanting nothing more
than that pound, pound, pound
When I toot that ass up, and you beat it down, down, down
and after I done sucked every last drop of nut out of you,
and you done licked ever centimeter of my ocean's floor
I'ma sit back and try to soak it all in
because when my high is gone
and you start to tarnish and fade,
and all your damn glitter went away.
And it just can't be a me and you

Him

I love it
sneaking
hiding
ducking
dodging
loving
touching
fucking
You
and don't nobody know
You kiss me like you want me
You hold me like...
You touch me like...
Right...
When I'm with you
You make me feel like there is nobody else
like this space
and the tongue tasting
and the heavy breathing
and hand placing
Is how it's supposed to be
You got me coming to see you,
Just to see you
Just to look at you
Just to watch you look at me and smile
I love the way your lips feel next to mine
How your body heat keeps me warm
The way you look at me
and the way you call me baby

Got me feeling
Special
And then you give me the prize
The monster with the one eye
You let me touch it
You let me suck it
I let you put it in
You let him fuck me
You make me cum on him
You let us both win
I'm glad I let you in
Because besides all that
I get to think about you
and I get to talk to you
Friends first, right
and I love that
I'm enjoying this ride before it ends
the part two of me and you
when I fall for him
and you fuck only on her
Damn I can't wait to see you again,
Soon

OUT

IT'S LIKE I'M
LOWERING MYSELF TO BE WITH YOU
I'M ACCUSTOM TO THE FINER THINGS IN LIFE
WHEN IT COMES TO DUDES
I PAY FOR NOTHING
I WANT FOR NOTHING
I'M BENEFITED
I'M UPGRADED
BUT WITH YOU I FEEL LIKE I'M BACK SLIDING
I'M PAYING TO BE WITH YOU
PAYING FOR DICK I DON'T EVEN WANT
BECAUSE IT'S NOT A GIFT
I SEE IT AS THE LEAST YOU CAN DO
YOU UP IN MY HOUSE
FEET ON MY COUCH
ASKING ME WHERE DINNER IS?
WHY THE HOUSE AIN'T CLEAN?
AS SOON AS I STEP IN
FROM WORKING A SHIFT OF FOURTEEN
HOURS
MINUTES
SECONDS
YOU HAVE BUT YOU WASTE THEM
HOW ARE YOU 30 AND STILL TRYING TO RAP?
WHO DOES THIS?
YOU SMOKE WEED WITH YOUR HOMEBOYS
GO HANG OUT ON THE BLOCK
SHOUTING OUT TO BITCHES
THAT YOU A BOSS

WHEN YOU NOT
EVERYTHING YOU HAVE, I GOT!!!
WHEN WE FIRST MET,
YOU WAS SELLING DREAMS
AND COULD KEEP THE PUSSY WET
SAID I WAS A PEARL,
A DOWN BITCH,
A BACKBONE TYPE OF GIRL
ALL YOU NEEDED WAS A LIL BOOST,
A LIL CUSHION TILL THIS MUSIC SHIT COME THRU
BBBBBBBBBBOOOOOO
MY NIGGA, I TELL YOU
IT'S LIKE YOU CONTENT ON BEING A BUM
I REFUSE TO DESTROY MY LIFE
BY THE LIKES OF YOU
EWWWWW
PLUS YOU STINK
IMA NEED YOU TO USE LOGIC WHEN YOU THINK
IT'S ONLY BEEN A WEEK
BUT I CAN SEE IT NOW
YOU TRYING TO DRIVE ME CRAZY IN MY OWN HOUSE
HURRY UP AND GET YOUR SHIT
BECAUSE I NEED YOU TO GET OUT

You

You.
You not the same no more
You use to be sweet
You used to be kind
You used to come and see me from time to time
I thought you were fine
I thought you were mine
I see now that you're not
I see a decision has been made
Your hand has been played
Game Over
Time Is up
And so is US.

Nyla

It's not that I didn't want you
I swear
I just couldn't give you what you needed
Trust me,
If me and your daddy would have been on the same page,
You would be here today
I was young
And he was dumb
He was in love with his past
And I was in love with my future
I know what it's like not to have a father around
I couldn't put you through that
I can only imagine how you would be
Good hair fa'sho
And pretty like me
With his eyes plus mine
We call that a dime
I sang to you before you left
I knew you would be sweet
Like a melody
Your daddy ain't all bad
He's a smart man
Very creative
It's just when I told him about you
He wasn't that elated
Even though I had him,
She had his heart
I would have taught you,
Don't trust these dudes

From the start
You're in a better place
And now I'm in a better place
So I can talk to you
Tell you, I'm sorry we never got to meet
Tell you, I never wanted you to leave
Tell you, you'll always be a part of me
Tell you, I will always love you
Nyla baby.

Bipolar

Kisses

No

Hug me

You won't

I don't want to talk to you

I do

I just wanna say

Even though I do,

I wish I didn't love you

I hate I'm thinking about you

When you only thinking about her

I feel stupid

My head hurts

Why are you here

In my mind

Get away from me

Wait come here,

No, I'll go

Why am I turning around?

I need you

I really don't

It's just...

I just

Miss you

HEAR ME

I JUST WANNA KNOW IF
WHEN I TALK
DO MY WORDS COME ACROSS
CLEARLY AND DIRECT
YOU KNOW HD LIKE
I WANNA KNOW IF YOU CAN HEAR ME
I'll SPEAK IN STEREO
NO MONOTONE
LET ME KNOW IF I'M TOO FAST
I'LL SAY IT SLOW
STACATTO
OR IF I'M TOO LOW
I'LL TURN IT UP
FALLSETTO
I REALLY WANT YOU TO FEEL IT
BELIEVE IT
VIBRATO
I'LL REPEAT IT IF I HAVE TO
I ECHO
THIS IS LAST TIME I'MA BE HERE
IN THIS SPACE
ALL IN YOUR FACE
SO TAKE HEED AND LISTEN TO ME BABY
THERE'S NO ENCORE
YOU READY
HERE IT GOES
I DON'T LOVE YOU
SO DON'T LOVE ME
KEPESH

Breakup/Love

Ok
Tonight is the night
I no longer put up a fight
I let go
I let us be
I take the me out of we
I can't
I don't wanna try
At times I wanna cry
That's not a good thing
Love is supposed to make me happy
I guess I was in love with the thought
of loving you
When you kissed me I felt anew
I wanted to make more of what the situation was
I know that I shouldn't
but
I wanna give you 110 percent
That's more than I give myself
The thought of having you around
for more than my usual takedowns
I guess I was so caught up
Holding on to our similarities
Holding on to the maybes
I forgot or I didn't want to see
that I'm not you
and you are not me
And right now the space
that it takes,

the time you must be willing to waste
to make a good thing work,
I'm not sure we ready for
At least not now
I'ma throw this love I thing I had for you
back into the universe
Let's see if it comes back
While we wait,
I wish you well
I want the best for you
until then ...
Much love always

Then

I was lost
nowhere to go
hurt and afraid
stuck
I shouldn't be here
There's no way I should be here right now
Should have AIDS
or 3kids
I should be crazy
My mind should be gone
My life should be way different
I'm supposed to be
another statistic
I'm supposed to be everything
they said I was
I'm supposed to be weak and defeated
Loveless and blind
I put myself in a lot of positions,
places, and situations
Things are supposed to be different,
but I was saved
I say saved because I didn't see
I couldn't see what was in front of me
I just knew I was tired of running
Tired of pretending to be someone I'm not
Tired of living the life that was expected of me
I was tired of being tired
Tired of heartache
Tired of being low

So I gave in
I surrendered my all
I had nothing left
So my all, my meaning my life, my mind, my heart
I had sense enough to know my way wasn't working
so let me just try it
I was ready
Opened myself, put it all out there
Forgave myself
Accepted that He forgave me
I didn't know what love was before
until I fell in love with Jesus
I have peace of mind
I know who I am
I have joy in my heart
If I never get famous or have no friends,
just having peace and joy is all worth it.
If he does nothing else for me,
I'm happy with that
I'm grateful
I'm humbled
and I'm great
I didn't know that before
I'm amazing, I couldn't say that before
For these reasons,
and this isn't half of them
I owe him my life
My life I owe
My ransom is my heart
My commitment is clear
to live how I was created to be

to be great in all that I do
and to put my heart into everything I do
my life no longer belongs to me
it is the Lord's
I might not get it right all the time
but I'm committed
I'm fully persuaded that this is my life
I am nothing without Jesus
And
He is Everything,
Everything,
Everything to me

Epic

That Night,
Was awesome
Drunken fun
Times only fantasies are made of
Sex, breast, and cum
Wild, crazy, dumb
Threesome
Plus one
All four
Blurred memory
Her and me
Him and we
Things we did
Produced consequences
We all paid for
I ain't been around
Ya'll seem to forget
I was the one you could talk to
About anything
Everything was exposed
Lies were told
Separation
Was it necessary?
Will we ever get it back to how it was?
Since when is busting a nut more important
Than common sense?
I haven't seen a condom since
Scared me straight
I watch who my mouth comes encounter with

I watch who I let hit
Black sheep
Who had it?
Who passed it?
Was it me?
Was it he?
We will never know the source
I'm grateful
Because it could have ended a different way
Pregnancy, HIV
Which is worse?
He say, She say
A secret I guess we taking it to our graves
We can repeat the story
Just as long as we don't mention names
One of the most memorable nights of my life
Is also the biggest curse
I guess that's what happens
When you do what you want to do,
Even though you know better
I'm well
Ya'll Facebook tell me you good
Lesson learned
Call me crazy,
But if we could do it again,
I would

Tell Me

What you gone do,
when I fall for you?
When all the games you play,
I let you win.
What are you going to do when I close my mouth?
When I let you in and when I let you play your position,
I let you lead the way?
Are you sure you want me?
All of me?
Because I give myself whole heartedly
You know I'm crazy right?
Crazy like psycho
Crazy like stalker
Crazy like anytime, anyplace
Crazy like no matter what you do, I just might stay
I'm a lot
I have a lot to offer
You know that right?
I'm flawed up too
I got stretch marks, I fart loud, and sometimes I have a bad attitude
I'ma ask you, Who is she?
I'ma want some attention
and other times I'm not going to even want to deal with you
Do you still want me boo?
I like you
I feel like you can tame me
I hope my past doesn't bother you
I'ma make you wait

You have to work for me
But I'm worth it
I'll be good to you
You have to be the cure to my nigga ADHD
You have to keep me focused
Tell me when I talk too much and to clean my room
I have a few other things
but most of all,
You have to do you
You can't be all up under me
You have to get your goals and your dreams accomplished
You have to be the man you were created to be
And still be there for me
That's a lot
I told you I'm crazy right?
I'm just telling you again,
so you know what you are getting yourself into
With all that being said,
Are you ready for me?
Because I'm ready for you
I'ma ask you my question again,
What are you going to do?

Truth

My desire is to be closer to you than ever before
I want to know you inside and out
I want to be all that you have created me to be
I want to be happy
I want to live my life with purpose
You saved me
I put myself in situations
and the only way I could get out,
was you
I can't go back to the old me
I only want to go higher
I'm willing to sacrifice
and do what I have to do get there
If that means I have to be all by myself to get closer to you,
I'll do that
I owe you my life
My life is yours
I have nothing
but you have everything in me
You have forgiven me
You have cleansed me
You have delivered me
You have changed me
I'm a different
I am new
I am yours
Help me to walk in that
Help me to really see and understand,
That you are

All
All

All I need in this life
and nothing else matters
Thank you

www.ingramcontent.com/pod-product-compliance
Lightning Source LLC
Chambersburg PA
CBHW062034040426
42447CB00010B/2279